gratitude journal for teens

the 90 day gratitude journal for teens

A TEENAGER'S GUIDE TO SELF DISCOVERY THROUGH JOURNALING, AFFIRMATIONS AND GRATITUDE

. . . .

NAME

dedicated to you, the teenager!

You are about to embark on an exciting journey to becoming more grateful, self aware and most of all, happier!

The pages in front of you will direct you in a positive direction by helping to **remind you of what you're grateful for**, what your **special talents are** and of the **good things and people you have in your life**.
It will guide you to build your dreams, plan positively-oriented states of mind, while helping you to navigate through some confusing teenage moods and emotions in a more productive and hopeful manner!

No matter who you are or what is going on around you, gratitude can help you live your life more fully, in small or big ways!

Improved Relationships

Greater Happiness

Higher Self Esteem

Better School Performance

gratitude

Gratitude is a positive emotion that involves being thankful and appreciative and is associated with several mental and health benefits.

SO WHAT DOES GRATITUDE LOOK LIKE?

When you experience gratitude, you feel grateful for something or someone in your life and respond with feelings of kindness, warmth and other forms of generosity. It is one of the healthiest and most positive emotions we can experience in our lives.

Gratitude helps you build a more satisfied and content mindset, making your life easier. In the morning it can set a positive tone for the day, and in the evening help you reflect back on the day and think of something good that happened. It will open your heart and help you through your stress and uncertainty about school, friends, social media and what the future holds.

Research has shown that being grateful physically changes our brains.

It boosts self-esteem, enhances empathy, and makes you sleep better. Gratitude also has the capacity to increase neuro-chemicals. When thinking shifts from negative to positive, there is a release of feel-good chemicals such as dopamine, serotonin and oxytocin that contribute to feelings of closeness, connection and happiness that come with gratitude.

Gratitude also helps to shift your attention away from toxic emotions such as resentment and envy. When you think about how grateful you are and how other people may have blessed your life, it is harder for you to ruminate on your negative experiences.

The mere act of writing about what you are grateful for can help you appreciate the people in your life more and help you take your focus away from negative feelings and thoughts.

Expressing gratitude contributes to greater mental health by increasing a positive outlook and lowering rates of stress and depression.

Positive Thinking

Lowers Anxiety

A sense of calm during scary times

Improved Sleep

JOURNALING

This is your space for free-style non-judgmental expression where you can process your thoughts, release your emotions, plan your days, and set your goals! You can write whatever you feel, or follow the prompts!

AFFIRMATIONS

This section is where you can write a short and positive statement about yourself, or a situation, that puts you in control of how you want to feel, or how you want a situation to go! You can write your own or use one of our suggestions. The more you say them, the better you feel!

GRATITUDE

This area is where you write about what, or who, you are grateful for. By thinking of three good things each day, you will build a positivity practice that opens your heart and leads you to greater happiness and resilience! It can be about something as little or as big as you want!

SELF CARE TIPS

These are coping suggestions we feature for you to use as needed. They are tips that help you feel better when you are having a hard day. You can follow ours, or come up with your own. The more coping skills you build, the more prepared you are in life! Think of them as your personal tool box!

how to use

DATE: M T W T F S S

fill in the date!

Today I am grateful for...

POSITIVE AFFIRMATION

WHAT I LEARNED TODAY

draw in your mood!

DISAPPOINTED SAD FRUSTRATED UNSURE OKAY HAPPY AWESOME

+ journaling page

I am amazing!

The things that make me different are the things that make me me.

I am not controlled by the opinions of others.

I believe in myself.

I am beautiful inside and out.

I am valuable.

I speak to myself with kindness.

I am allowed to feel proud of myself.

I don't compare myself to others: I am unique and amazing.

I am kind and smart and important.

I can reach my dreams.

My opinion matters.

I trust my decisions and the instincts that I have.

affirmations

I listen to others with kindness and an open mind.

I can reach my dreams.

I don't need to be perfect to be accepted.

I am good enough exactly as I am.

I deserve to be happy.

I can make mistakes and still be loved.

I am safe and secure.

I can persevere and do hard things.

I am strong.

I trust myself.

I love and approve of myself.

My hopes and dreams are important and should be heard.

DATE: M T W T F S S

Today I am grateful for...

POSITIVE AFFIRMATION

WHAT I LEARNED TODAY

DISAPPOINTED SAD FRUSTRATED UNSURE OKAY HAPPY AWESOME

HAVE YOU EVER HAD TO HAVE A REALLY DIFFICULT CONVERSATION WITH SOMEONE? HOW DID YOU HANDLE IT?

Thoughts...

DATE:

M T W T F S S

Today I am grateful for...

POSITIVE AFFIRMATION

WHAT I LEARNED TODAY

WHAT BRINGS YOU THE MOST JOY?

Thoughts...

DATE: M T W T F S S

Today I am grateful for...

POSITIVE AFFIRMATION

WHAT I LEARNED TODAY

DISAPPOINTED SAD FRUSTRATED UNSURE OKAY HAPPY AWESOME

YOU HAVE TO RELIVE AN ENTIRE YEAR OF YOUR LIFE. WHICH YEAR WOULD YOU PICK?

Thoughts...

DATE: M T W T F S S

Today I am grateful for...

POSITIVE AFFIRMATION

WHAT I LEARNED TODAY

DISAPPOINTED SAD FRUSTRATED UNSURE OKAY HAPPY AWESOME

WHAT IS SOMETHING THAT YOU BELIEVE IN STRONGLY?

Thoughts...

DATE: M T W T F S S

Today I am grateful for...

POSITIVE AFFIRMATION

WHAT I LEARNED TODAY

DISAPPOINTED SAD FRUSTRATED UNSURE OKAY HAPPY AWESOME

DO YOU PREFER TO BE IN THE SPOTLIGHT OR BEHIND THE SCENES?

Thoughts...

DATE: M T W T F S S

Today I am grateful for...

POSITIVE AFFIRMATION

WHAT I LEARNED TODAY

DISAPPOINTED SAD FRUSTRATED UNSURE OKAY HAPPY AWESOME

IF YOU COULD LIVE IN THE FICTIONAL WORLD OF ANY BOOK OR SERIES, WHICH ONE WOULD YOU CHOOSE AND WHY?

Thoughts...

DATE: M T W T F S S

Today I am grateful for...

POSITIVE AFFIRMATION

WHAT I LEARNED TODAY

DISAPPOINTED SAD FRUSTRATED UNSURE OKAY HAPPY AWESOME

IF YOU COULD CHANGE THREE THINGS ABOUT THE WORLD, WHAT WOULD YOU CHANGE AND WHY?

Thoughts...

i am unique and there is no one with my exact talents

tip 1

POSITIVE SELF TALK

Catch negative thoughts when they start and REFRAME it to something positive.

DATE: M T W T F S S

Today I am grateful for...

POSITIVE AFFIRMATION

WHAT I LEARNED TODAY

WHAT WOULD YOUR DREAM HOUSE LOOK LIKE? WHERE WOULD IT BE?

Thoughts...

DATE: M T W T F S S

Today I am grateful for...

POSITIVE AFFIRMATION

WHAT I LEARNED TODAY

DISAPPOINTED SAD FRUSTRATED UNSURE OKAY HAPPY AWESOME

DESCRIBE YOUR BEST SUMMER VACATION MEMORY.

Thoughts...

DATE: M T W T F S S

Today I am grateful for...

POSITIVE AFFIRMATION

WHAT I LEARNED TODAY

DISAPPOINTED SAD FRUSTRATED UNSURE OKAY HAPPY AWESOME

WHAT IS YOUR GREATEST ACCOMPLISHMENT SO FAR?

Thoughts...

DATE: M T W T F S S

Today I am grateful for...

POSITIVE AFFIRMATION

WHAT I LEARNED TODAY

DISAPPOINTED SAD FRUSTRATED UNSURE OKAY HAPPY AWESOME

WRITE A LIST OF QUESTIONS TO YOUR OLDER SELF.

Thoughts...

there are always flowers for those who want to see them

tip 4

DRINK WATER

Hydrate first thing in the morning and throughout the day.

DATE: M T W T F S S

Today I am grateful for...

POSITIVE AFFIRMATION

WHAT I LEARNED TODAY

DISAPPOINTED SAD FRUSTRATED UNSURE OKAY HAPPY AWESOME

WHAT IS YOUR EARLIEST MEMORY?

Thoughts...

DATE:

M T W T F S S

Today I am grateful for...

POSITIVE AFFIRMATION

WHAT I LEARNED TODAY

DISAPPOINTED SAD FRUSTRATED UNSURE OKAY HAPPY AWESOME

ARE YOU WISELY USING YOUR TIME?

Thoughts...

DATE: M T W T F S S

Today I am grateful for...

POSITIVE AFFIRMATION

WHAT I LEARNED TODAY

DISAPPOINTED SAD FRUSTRATED UNSURE OKAY HAPPY AWESOME

WHAT SITUATIONS MAKE YOU THE MOST FEARFUL?

Thoughts...

DATE:

M T W T F S S

Today I am grateful for...

POSITIVE AFFIRMATION

WHAT I LEARNED TODAY

DO YOU HAVE A GOOD SUPPORT SYSTEM FOR YOUR ANXIETY? WHY?

Thoughts...

DATE: M T W T F S S

Today I am grateful for...

POSITIVE AFFIRMATION

WHAT I LEARNED TODAY

DISAPPOINTED SAD FRUSTRATED UNSURE OKAY HAPPY AWESOME

HOW DO YOU DEAL WITH STRESS DIFFERENTLY NOW THAN WHEN YOU WERE YOUNGER?

Thoughts...

DATE: M T W T F S S

Today I am grateful for...

POSITIVE AFFIRMATION

WHAT I LEARNED TODAY

DISAPPOINTED SAD FRUSTRATED UNSURE OKAY HAPPY AWESOME

SHARE GRATITUDE FOR THREE PEOPLE WHO ARE SUPPORTING YOU AT THIS POINT IN YOUR LIFE.

Thoughts...

DATE: M T W T F S S

Today I am grateful for...

POSITIVE AFFIRMATION

WHAT I LEARNED TODAY

DISAPPOINTED SAD FRUSTRATED UNSURE OKAY HAPPY AWESOME

WHAT IS ONE THING ABOUT TODAY THAT SURPRISED YOU?

Thoughts...

if you want to find happiness, find gratitude.

tip 5

BREATHE DEEPLY

Take a deep breath and practice breathing throughout the day.

DATE: M T W T F S S

Today I am grateful for...

POSITIVE AFFIRMATION

WHAT I LEARNED TODAY

DISAPPOINTED SAD FRUSTRATED UNSURE OKAY HAPPY AWESOME

WHAT'S ONE GOAL OR CHALLENGE YOU HAVE FOR YOURSELF THIS WEEK? HOW WILL YOU ACCOMPLISH IT?

Thoughts...

DATE: M T W T F S S

Today I am grateful for...

POSITIVE AFFIRMATION

WHAT I LEARNED TODAY

DISAPPOINTED SAD FRUSTRATED UNSURE OKAY HAPPY AWESOME

THINK ABOUT YOUR FAVORITE HOBBY OR ACTIVITY. WHY DO YOU LOVE IT?

Thoughts...

DATE: M T W T F S S

Today I am grateful for...

. . . .

. . . .

. . . .

. . . .

. . . .

. . . .

. . . .

POSITIVE AFFIRMATION

WHAT I LEARNED TODAY

. . . .

. . . .

. . . .

. . . .

DISAPPOINTED SAD FRUSTRATED UNSURE OKAY HAPPY AWESOME

WHAT'S ONE THING THAT ALWAYS MAKES YOU LAUGH?

Thoughts...

DATE:

M T W T F S S

Today I am grateful for...

POSITIVE AFFIRMATION

WHAT I LEARNED TODAY

DISAPPOINTED SAD FRUSTRATED UNSURE OKAY HAPPY AWESOME

CLOSE YOUR EYES AND LISTEN TO THE WORLD AROUND YOU. WHAT SOUNDS DO YOU HEAR? WRITE THEM DOWN.

Thoughts...

DATE: M T W T F S S

Today I am grateful for...

POSITIVE AFFIRMATION

WHAT I LEARNED TODAY

DISAPPOINTED SAD FRUSTRATED UNSURE OKAY HAPPY AWESOME

HAVE YOU EVER WANTED TO LEARN ANOTHER LANGUAGE? WHAT WOULD YOU WANT TO LEARN?

Thoughts...

WHAT IS YOUR FAVORITE THING ABOUT YOURSELF?

Thoughts...

no one has
ever become
poor by
giving

tip 7

PRACTICE KINDNESS

Say hello to a stranger or help a person in need.

DATE:

M T W T F S S

Today I am grateful for...

POSITIVE AFFIRMATION

WHAT I LEARNED TODAY

DISAPPOINTED SAD FRUSTRATED UNSURE OKAY HAPPY AWESOME

WHAT IS ONE OF YOUR FUNNIEST MEMORIES?

Thoughts...

DATE: M T W T F S S

Today I am grateful for...

POSITIVE AFFIRMATION

WHAT I LEARNED TODAY

DISAPPOINTED SAD FRUSTRATED UNSURE OKAY HAPPY AWESOME

THINK ABOUT YOUR FAVORITE COLOR. WHAT DOES IT REMIND YOU OF?

Thoughts...

DATE: M T W T F S S

Today I am grateful for...

POSITIVE AFFIRMATION

WHAT I LEARNED TODAY

DISAPPOINTED SAD FRUSTRATED UNSURE OKAY HAPPY AWESOME

WHO IS SOMEONE YOU MISS? WHAT WOULD YOU SAY TO THEM IF THEY WERE NEXT TO YOU RIGHT NOW?

Thoughts...

DATE: M T W T F S S

Today I am grateful for...

POSITIVE AFFIRMATION

WHAT I LEARNED TODAY

DISAPPOINTED SAD FRUSTRATED UNSURE OKAY HAPPY AWESOME

WHAT'S ONE THING YOU'VE NEVER TOLD ANYONE BEFORE?

Thoughts...

DATE: M T W T F S S

Today I am grateful for...

POSITIVE AFFIRMATION

WHAT I LEARNED TODAY

DISAPPOINTED SAD FRUSTRATED UNSURE OKAY HAPPY AWESOME

DO YOU HAVE A FAVORITE QUOTE? WRITE IT DOWN HERE. WHY IS IT YOUR FAVORITE?

Thoughts...

DATE:

M T W T F S S

Today I am grateful for...

POSITIVE AFFIRMATION

WHAT I LEARNED TODAY

DISAPPOINTED SAD FRUSTRATED UNSURE OKAY HAPPY AWESOME

WHAT DO YOU LOVE ABOUT YOUR FAMILY?

Thoughts...

DATE: M T W T F S S

Today I am grateful for...

POSITIVE AFFIRMATION

WHAT I LEARNED TODAY

DISAPPOINTED SAD FRUSTRATED UNSURE OKAY HAPPY AWESOME

DO YOU REMEMBER YOUR FIRST DAY OF SCHOOL? WHAT WAS IT LIKE?

Thoughts...

be happy for
this moment

tip 8

GET SUPPORT

Talk to a friend and reduce worry about things you can't control.

DATE:

M T W T F S S

Today I am grateful for...

POSITIVE AFFIRMATION

WHAT I LEARNED TODAY

IF YOU COULD TALK TO YOUR PAST SELF, WHAT WOULD YOU SAY?

Thoughts...

DATE: M T W T F S S

Today I am grateful for...

POSITIVE AFFIRMATION

WHAT I LEARNED TODAY

DISAPPOINTED SAD FRUSTRATED UNSURE OKAY HAPPY AWESOME

WHAT IS ONE THING YOU'RE EXCITED ABOUT? WHY?

Thoughts...

DATE:

M T W T F S S

Today I am grateful for...

POSITIVE AFFIRMATION

WHAT I LEARNED TODAY

DISAPPOINTED SAD FRUSTRATED UNSURE OKAY HAPPY AWESOME

IF YOU COULD HAVE ANY SUPERPOWER, WHICH ONE WOULD YOU CHOOSE? WHAT WOULD YOU DO WITH IT?

Thoughts...

DATE: M T W T F S S

Today I am grateful for...

. . . .

. . . .

. . . .

. . . .

. . . .

. . . .

. . . .

POSITIVE AFFIRMATION

WHAT I LEARNED TODAY

. . . .

. . . .

. . . .

. . . .

DISAPPOINTED SAD FRUSTRATED UNSURE OKAY HAPPY AWESOME

WHAT'S THE BEST WAY TO SPEND A RAINY DAY?

Thoughts...

DATE:

M T W T F S S

Today I am grateful for...

POSITIVE AFFIRMATION

WHAT I LEARNED TODAY

DISAPPOINTED SAD FRUSTRATED UNSURE OKAY HAPPY AWESOME

WRITE DOWN THREE WAYS YOU COULD HELP A FRIEND OR FAMILY MEMBER.

Thoughts...

DATE:

M T W T F S S

Today I am grateful for...

POSITIVE AFFIRMATION

WHAT I LEARNED TODAY

DISAPPOINTED SAD FRUSTRATED UNSURE OKAY HAPPY AWESOME

WRITE ABOUT THREE PLACES YOU WOULD LIKE TO TRAVEL SOMEDAY. WHAT DO THESE THREE PLACES HAVE IN COMMON?

Thoughts...

DATE:

M T W T F S S

Today I am grateful for...

POSITIVE AFFIRMATION

WHAT I LEARNED TODAY

DISAPPOINTED SAD FRUSTRATED UNSURE OKAY HAPPY AWESOME

IF YOU WERE IN CHARGE OF THE WHOLE WORLD, WHAT WOULD YOU DO TO MAKE THE WORLD A HAPPIER PLACE?

Thoughts...

kindness always comes back

tip 09

GIVE

Join a community or volunteer in your area.

DATE: M T W T F S S

Today I am grateful for...

POSITIVE AFFIRMATION

WHAT I LEARNED TODAY

DISAPPOINTED SAD FRUSTRATED UNSURE OKAY HAPPY AWESOME

WHO MAKES YOU FEEL LOVED? WHAT DO THEY DO OR SAY TO MAKE YOU FEEL LOVED?

Thoughts...

DATE: M T W T F S S

Today I am grateful for...

POSITIVE AFFIRMATION

WHAT I LEARNED TODAY

DISAPPOINTED SAD FRUSTRATED UNSURE OKAY HAPPY AWESOME

DESCRIBE A MISTAKE YOU MADE AND HOW YOU LEARNED FROM IT.

Thoughts...

DATE:

M T W T F S S

Today I am grateful for...

POSITIVE AFFIRMATION

WHAT I LEARNED TODAY

DISAPPOINTED SAD FRUSTRATED UNSURE OKAY HAPPY AWESOME

WHAT ASPECT OF YOUR FAMILY BRINGS OUT THE BEST IN YOU?

Thoughts...

DATE:

M T W T F S S

Today I am grateful for...

POSITIVE AFFIRMATION

WHAT I LEARNED TODAY

DISAPPOINTED SAD FRUSTRATED UNSURE OKAY HAPPY AWESOME

WHAT CHALLENGES YOU ABOUT YOUR FAMILY?

Thoughts...

DATE: M T W T F S S

Today I am grateful for...

POSITIVE AFFIRMATION

WHAT I LEARNED TODAY

DISAPPOINTED SAD FRUSTRATED UNSURE OKAY HAPPY AWESOME

WRITE ABOUT SOMETHING YOU DIDN'T THINK YOU COULD DO BUT MANAGED TO DO.

Thoughts...

DATE: M T W T F S S

Today I am grateful for...

POSITIVE AFFIRMATION

WHAT I LEARNED TODAY

DISAPPOINTED SAD FRUSTRATED UNSURE OKAY HAPPY AWESOME

WHICH OF YOUR QUALITIES DO YOU THINK YOU SHOULD WORK ON IMPROVING?

Thoughts...

DATE: M T W T F S S

Today I am grateful for...

. . . .

. . . .

. . . .

. . . .

. . . .

. . . .

. . . .

POSITIVE AFFIRMATION

WHAT I LEARNED TODAY

. . . .

. . . .

. . . .

. . . .

WHAT IS YOUR BIGGEST GOAL IN LIFE?

Thoughts...

your patience
is your
power

tip 10

A.M PHONE DETOX

Take a break and get through the morning without reaching for the phone.

DATE: M T W T F S S

Today I am grateful for...

POSITIVE AFFIRMATION

WHAT I LEARNED TODAY

DISAPPOINTED SAD FRUSTRATED UNSURE OKAY HAPPY AWESOME

WHERE IS THE MOST INTERESTING PLACE YOU HAVE EVER BEEN TO?

Thoughts...

DATE:

M T W T F S S

Today I am grateful for...

POSITIVE AFFIRMATION

WHAT I LEARNED TODAY

DISAPPOINTED SAD FRUSTRATED UNSURE OKAY HAPPY AWESOME

WHO IS THE FUNNIEST PERSON YOU KNOW? WHY?

Thoughts...

DATE: M T W T F S S

Today I am grateful for...

POSITIVE AFFIRMATION

WHAT I LEARNED TODAY

DISAPPOINTED SAD FRUSTRATED UNSURE OKAY HAPPY AWESOME

DESCRIBE THE BEST GIFT YOU EVER RECEIVED.

Thoughts...

DATE: M T W T F S S

Today I am grateful for...

POSITIVE AFFIRMATION

WHAT I LEARNED TODAY

DISAPPOINTED SAD FRUSTRATED UNSURE OKAY HAPPY AWESOME

WHAT ARE THE QUALITIES A BEST FRIEND SHOULD HAVE?

Thoughts...

Thoughts...

Thoughts...

Thoughts...

Thoughts...

Thoughts...

Thoughts...

Thoughts...

Made in the USA
Columbia, SC
21 June 2023

18533179R00117